Specific Skill Series
for Reading

Finding Details

Sixth Edition

Columbus, OH

The **McGraw·Hill** *Companies*

Cover: © Randy Faris/Corbis

SRAonline.com

 SRA

Send all inquiries to:
SRA/McGraw-Hill
4400 Easton Commons
Columbus, OH 43219

ISBN 0-07-603996-X

3 4 5 6 7 8 9 BCH 12 11 10 09 08 07

PURPOSE:

FINDING DETAILS is designed to develop skill in recalling details from a single reading. The material is structured so students cannot "look back" for the answer. The story is on one side; the questions are on the reverse. Readers must take as much as they can from one reading. The knowledge that they cannot turn back to the story helps them gain skill in **FINDING DETAILS.**

FOR WHOM:

The skill of **FINDING DETAILS** is developed through a series of books spanning ten levels (Picture, Preparatory, A, B, C, D, E, F, G, H). The Picture Level is for students who have not acquired a basic sight vocabulary. The Preparatory Level is for students who have a basic sight vocabulary but are not quite ready for the first-grade-level book. Books A through H are appropriate for students who can read on levels one through eight, respectively.

THE NEW EDITION:

The sixth edition of the *Specific Skill Series for Reading* maintains the quality and focus that has distinguished this program for more than 40 years. A key element central to the program's success has been the unique nature of the reading selections. Fiction and nonfiction pieces about current topics have been designed to stimulate the interest of students, motivating them to use the comprehension strategies they have learned to further their reading. To keep this important aspect of the program intact, a percentage of the reading selections has been replaced in order to ensure the continued relevance of the subject material.

In addition, a significant percentage of the artwork in the program has been replaced to give the books a contemporary look. The cover photographs are designed to appeal to readers of all ages.

SESSIONS:

Short practice sessions are the most effective. It is desirable to have a practice session every day or every other day, using a few units each session.

SCORING:

Students should record their answers on the reproducible worksheets. The worksheets make scoring easier and provide uniform records of the students' work. Using worksheets also avoids consuming the exercise books.

TO THE TEACHER

It is important for students to know how well they are doing. For this reason, units should be scored as soon as they have been completed. Then a discussion can be held in which students justify their choices. (The *Language Activity Pages,* many of which are open-ended, do not lend themselves to an objective score; thus there are no answer keys for these pages.)

GENERAL INFORMATION ON *FINDING DETAILS:*

FINDING DETAILS varies in content. It contains both fiction and nonfiction stories that will help stretch the imagination, spark new hobbies, promote admiration for outstanding achievements, and develop a sense of wonder about our world.

There is only one correct answer for each question. Students practice recalling details they read or saw in a picture. **FINDING DETAILS** helps students' comprehension as they carefully read and answer each question with the statement that correctly states a detail found in the selection.

SUGGESTED STEPS:

1. Students read the story. (In the Picture Level books, the students look at the pictures.)

2. After completing the story, students turn to the questions on the reverse side and choose the letters of the correct answers.

3. Students write the letters of the correct answers on the worksheets.

4. Students may return to the story only after their answers have been recorded and scored.

RELATED MATERIALS:

Specific Skill Series Assessment Book provides the teacher with a pretest and a posttest for each skill at each grade level. These tests will help the teacher assess the students' performance in each of the nine comprehension skills.

About This Book

A **detail** is additional information about what you are reading. Details help you visualize what a writer is describing. Being able to recall details will help you with other reading skills.

- Earth is 92.9 million miles from the sun.
- George Washington was born on February 22, 1732.

There are details in everything you read. Read this paragraph:

There are trees that really "walk." They grow in Florida. These trees have long roots that reach out like legs. As the roots grow out, they pull the tree along.

These are details from the paragraph:

- There are trees that walk.
- They grow in Florida.
- They have long roots that reach out like legs.
- The roots pull the tree along.

Reading a selection for details is not the same as reading a story just for fun. You should read more slowly when you are reading to find out new information. To understand the information, you may need to figure out the meanings of new words. To remember the details, you may need to read part of the article again.

In this book, you will read selections on many different subjects. After you have read a selection, turn the page to find ten questions about it. The incorrect answers may be true and make sense, but the only correct answer choice is the one that is stated in the selection. "Finding Details" means getting the details from a particular selection. Only by reading the selection carefully can you answer the questions correctly.

CONTENTS

Unit 1
Salty Waters

Can you imagine water so thick that you would float with no effort at all? This water exists! The thick water is in the Dead Sea, a salt lake that lies on the border between Israel and Jordan. It is set in a deep valley, with golden-brown walls rising 4,000 feet above it.

From the air the Dead Sea looks like a sparkling blue lake about fifty miles long and ten miles wide. It contains the saltiest water on Earth. It is so salty that few people would care to swim in it.

The Dead Sea is so salty that no fish or plants can live in it. One legend says that the air above the Dead Sea will kill birds that fly overhead. That's not true. The air above the Dead Sea is perfectly safe. However, few birds would bother to fly over it—after all, it contains nothing for them to eat!

How did the Dead Sea get to be so salty? Imagine fresh water flowing into a lake. Once the water is in the lake, it has nowhere to go because the lake is at the lowest point on Earth. Then imagine the sun beating down. Some of the water evaporates, or changes from a liquid into a gas. The water started out with tiny amounts of salt in it. Almost all water has some salt, which it picks up from the ground. Now imagine this process happening for thousands of years. The water keeps coming in and then evaporating. The salt stays behind. The water that stays behind grows more and more salty.

What good is the Dead Sea if nothing grows in it and nobody goes there for vacation? The edges of the sea contain some valuable minerals. These are dug up and sold.

1. The water in the Dead Sea is very
   (A) thin.　　　　　　(B) thick.　　　　　　(C) cold.

2. Swimmers in the Dead Sea would
   (A) float.　　　　　　(B) sink.　　　　　　(C) sing.

3. This is because the Dead Sea contains a lot of
   (A) ice.　　　　　　(B) dirt.　　　　　　(C) salt.

4. From the air the Dead Sea looks like a
   (A) pile of salt.　　　　(B) blue lake.　　　　(C) huge ocean.

5. The Dead Sea is about
   (A) 10 miles long.　　(B) 4,000 feet deep.　(C) 50 miles long.

6. The Dead Sea contains no
   (A) water or rocks.　　(B) salt.　　　　(C) fish or plants.

7. A bird flying over the Dead Sea would
   (A) be killed.　　　　(B) find no food.　　(C) see no water.

8. Fresh water contains tiny amounts of
   (A) iron.　　　　　　(B) animals.　　　　(C) salt.

9. When water evaporates, salt
   (A) stays behind.　　(B) also evaporates.　(C) turns to stone.

10. The edges of the Dead Sea contain
    (A) gold.　　　　　　(B) minerals.　　　　(C) trees.

Unit 2
The Beautiful Road

Today we repair or replace roads every few years. The Inca civilization built their road system to last. And they built it more than 500 years ago.

The Inca civilization was in the Andes Mountains in South America. They lived in what is now Peru. Their empire stretched for thousands of miles. They went everywhere on foot, so they built 5,000 miles of roadway.

The main Inca road was called Capac Nan. This means "Beautiful Road." It was paved and had gutters and curbs. It was lined with trees to provide shade for travelers. The road went along high mountain ridges, through deep valleys, and across bridges over rivers.

The main branch of Capac Nan covered the same distance as that from London to New York. Much of the system is crumbling today, but some parts of it can still be traveled in comfort.

The Incas used their road to get important news to all parts of their empire. The news was delivered by runners. The runners were trained from the time they were children. They had to learn to run fast at high altitudes with little oxygen.

The runners were set up in relay systems. Each one would run about two miles and then give his news to the next runner. The runners could cover about 250 miles each day. This is about the same rate as the Pony Express traveled in the United States. But the Pony Express used—you guessed it—horses!

Unit 2
The Beautiful Road

1. The Inca people lived in the
   (A) Andes.   (B) Rockies.   (C) Alps.

2. The country of Peru is in
   (A) Europe.   (B) South America.   (C) England.

3. The Incas traveled on
   (A) carts.   (B) foot.   (C) boats.

4. Trees were planted along the road to provide
   (A) fruit.   (B) firewood.   (C) shade.

5. The Inca road covered thousands of
   (A) miles.   (B) valleys.   (C) gutters.

6. The Incas delivered news by
   (A) runners.   (B) horse.   (C) radio.

7. The runners started their training as
   (A) teenagers.   (B) children.   (C) adults.

8. At high altitudes there was little
   (A) oxygen.   (B) shelter.   (C) food.

9. Each runner would pass his news to the next runner after two
   (A) miles.   (B) days.   (C) naps.

10. The Inca runner system could cover 250 miles each
    (A) week.   (B) day.   (C) hour.

Unit 3
The Biggest Creature of All

Can you name the largest animal that has ever lived? Is it the elephant? Or is it the extinct animal of long ago, the dinosaur? If you chose either one, you're wrong. The largest animal that has ever lived on Earth is alive today. It is the great blue whale.

An adult blue whale is longer than two city buses. Its heart is the size of a taxicab. The whale can weigh as much as 170,000 tons. To feed its enormous body, the blue whale takes in 45 tons of water per gulp. It then strains the water through hundreds of bony plates to take out three to four tons of krill, its food, each day.

Blubber is a whale's fat. In the blue whale the blubber may equal one third of the animal's total weight. The blubber is rich in oil, which is why people have hunted the blue whale for so long.

Surprisingly, though the blue whale is huge, it is not slow. It was able to outrun sailing ships for 300 years. Then steamships allowed whale hunters to catch up to the giant. So many blue whales were killed that the species almost became extinct. Now blue whales are protected, and biologists believe they are making a comeback.

Scientists have reported seeing blue whales off the California coast. These whales are not as easy to find as those that sing, jump, or travel in large packs, thus, anyone who does spot a blue whale thinks the day has been a success.

Unit 3
The Biggest Creature of All

1. The largest animal that has ever lived is the
 (A) dinosaur. **(B)** elephant. **(C)** blue whale.

2. The largest animal that has ever lived is
 (A) on land. **(B)** alive today. **(C)** not living today.

3. The blue whale is longer than
 (A) two city buses. **(B)** ten trains. **(C)** a mile.

4. In one gulp the blue whale takes in water at the rate of
 (A) 170 tons. **(B)** 45 tons. **(C)** 4 tons.

5. The blue whale eats
 (A) blubber. **(B)** oil. **(C)** krill.

6. Blubber is a whale's
 (A) fat. **(B)** skin. **(C)** fins.

7. People have hunted the blue whale for its
 (A) oil. **(B)** krill. **(C)** song.

8. It surprises people to learn that the huge blue whale is
 (A) fast. **(B)** fat. **(C)** sleepy.

9. Whalers started catching blue whales after they had
 (A) submarines. **(B)** steamships. **(C)** canoes.

10. Blue whale numbers are increasing because they are
 (A) having twins. **(B)** hunted. **(C)** protected.

Icebergs develop in the coldest parts of the world. There the land is covered with ice. The ice moves slowly over the land to the sea. The waves of the sea break off huge pieces of ice. These pieces are new icebergs.

Not all icebergs are the same size. Some are only 20 or 30 feet long. Others are as large as mountains. The largest icebergs are 70 or even 80 miles long. These icy giants may reach 500 feet into the sky. This is as high as a 50-story building. No wonder icebergs are often called "floating giants."

We can see only a small part of an iceberg. Most of it is hidden underwater. The part underwater is nine times as large as the part above the water. That is why a ship can never sail too close to an iceberg. The part of the iceberg hidden underwater could rip open the bottom of the ship and make it sink. Icebergs have also been known to roll over. Who would want to be caught underneath? An iceberg may weigh as much as 10,000 elephants!

Icebergs may exist for many years. Those that float around in the coldest water often last for 50 or even 100 years. Those icebergs that drift into warmer waters don't last as long. They melt after only a few years.

The great white mountains of ice split in two when they melt. Cracking icebergs sound like thunder. The sound can be heard many miles away. Perhaps it is the floating giant's way of saying, "Get one last look, everybody. I'm starting to melt!"

Unit 4
Floating Giants

1. Icebergs form where the land is covered with
   (A) ice. (B) water. (C) boats.

2. Ice moves over the land
   (A) quickly. (B) slowly. (C) sadly.

3. Large pieces of ice are broken off by
   (A) waves. (B) wind. (C) whales.

4. Icebergs are
   (A) small. (B) not all the same size. (C) mountains.

5. The longest icebergs are
   (A) eight feet. (B) eight miles. (C) 80 miles.

6. Most of an iceberg is
   (A) growing. (B) hidden. (C) above the water.

7. In very cold water, icebergs may exist for
   (A) a few years. (B) 100 years. (C) 500 years.

8. Icebergs that drift into warm water may exist
   (A) a few years. (B) 100 years. (C) forever.

9. When icebergs melt they often split
   (A) into five pieces. (B) in front. (C) in two.

10. When icebergs split it sounds like
    (A) waves. (B) thunder. (C) babies.

Unit 5
Funny Money

Money! What do you see when you hear this word? Do you picture a round metal coin? Do you think of paper money? Most likely you think of one or the other. The money we see or use is made of paper or metal. But the money of long ago was not at all like the money we use today.

Coins were not always made of metal. Soap was once used as money by the people of Mexico. Lumps of coal were used as coins by the people of England. Stone money was used on the Pacific Ocean island of Yap.

Even food was used as money. In Russia coins of cheese could be used to buy things. Bricks of tea leaves were used as money in Tibet. The tea leaves were first boiled in water. They were then pressed into hard brick shapes.

Coins were not always round. The coins of old China were once in the shape of a knife. In another land coins were made in the shape of a fish. Square money is still used by the people of India. Money in shapes of rings and bracelets is also still seen in some parts of the world, making it easy to carry.

Did you ever hear anyone say, "Money doesn't grow on trees"? Is it true? Did money ever grow on trees? In far-off Malaysia, people once made their own small trees out of tin. Small, round tin coins were joined to the trunk of the tin-money trees. People just broke off the money they needed. Wouldn't it be nice if people had money trees of their own?

Unit 5
Funny Money

1. The money we see and use today is made of
   (A) wood.
   (B) gold.
   (C) paper or metal.

2. Soap was once used as money by the people of
   (A) Mexico.
   (B) Canada.
   (C) Ireland.

3. People in England once used money made of
   (A) coffee.
   (B) sugar.
   (C) coal.

4. Stone money was used by the people of
   (A) India.
   (B) England.
   (C) Yap.

5. In Russia coins were once made of
   (A) monkeys.
   (B) cheese.
   (C) bread.

6. Before tea leaves were made into money, they were
   (A) eaten.
   (B) baked.
   (C) boiled.

7. Coins of old China were once made in the shape of
   (A) knives.
   (B) sheep.
   (C) cars.

8. In India we can still find
   (A) wet money.
   (B) fat coins.
   (C) square coins.

9. Ring money is easy to
   (A) make.
   (B) carry.
   (C) eat.

10. The people of one country once made
    (A) money trees.
    (B) money games.
    (C) stones.

Unit 6
How to Get There from Here

You know how important a map is to show you where things are. Early civilizations thought maps were important too. The oldest map on record gives the outline of a person's estate. Perhaps he wanted everyone to know which land was his.

Mapmaking became more important when people started exploring. If travelers kept maps of where they had been, the trip would be easier for the next person. Unfortunately, early maps were not very scientific. People did not know what lay across the seas or over the next mountain. They imagined the seas to be full of monsters that would sink ships. Often a mapmaker would draw these so-called monsters right on a map.

Early maps were made from common materials. The arctic people used both dark- and light-colored animal skins. They cut the shape of their islands from the dark skins. Then they sewed the shapes to the large, light skin, representing the ocean. South Pacific islanders used shells and bits of coral to represent their islands on maps.

Early mapmakers disagreed about which directions were important. Some put east at the top of their maps, because the sun rises from that direction. Others put the direction of the prevailing winds at the top because winds were very important to sailors.

In the second century A.D., an Egyptian named Ptolemy began to improve mapmaking. He moved it from art into science. First he put north at the top of his maps. And, as an astronomer, he based his maps on a round Earth. He tried to make the distances between lands on a map more accurate. Ptolemy's maps were so good that they were still used hundreds of years after his death.

Unit 6
How to Get There from Here

1. The earliest recorded map shows a person's
   - **(A)** ship.
   - **(B)** island.
   - **(C)** estate.

2. Mapmaking became more important because of
   - **(A)** drawing.
   - **(B)** exploration.
   - **(C)** astronomy.

3. Early maps were not very
   - **(A)** artistic.
   - **(B)** interesting.
   - **(C)** scientific.

4. Some people imagined that ships were sunk by
   - **(A)** monsters.
   - **(B)** storms.
   - **(C)** rocks.

5. The arctic people used dark animal skins to represent
   - **(A)** the oceans.
   - **(B)** islands.
   - **(C)** monsters.

6. Early mapmakers had different ideas about
   - **(A)** direction.
   - **(B)** winds.
   - **(C)** sailing.

7. Some thought east was the most important because of
   - **(A)** sunset.
   - **(B)** sunrises.
   - **(C)** eclipses.

8. The direction of the prevailing winds was important to
   - **(A)** sailors.
   - **(B)** islanders.
   - **(C)** artists.

9. Ptolemy's map skills grew from his work as an
   - **(A)** Egyptian.
   - **(B)** astronomer.
   - **(C)** Inuit.

10. Ptolemy determined that the direction at the top of the map should be
    - **(A)** north.
    - **(B)** east.
    - **(C)** winds.

The First L A P
Language Activity Pages

In Unit 5 you read about different kinds of money. Some money is made of metal, but other money has been made from stone, coal, tea, and even cheese. Think about the money you use. What is it made of? What colors and shapes does it have? Then read the following paragraph about money.

Money is a useful tool for buying things. Without money we would have to use other things—work, products we had made, or foods we had grown—to trade for things we wanted. What makes money work? Money must have a value of its own. Some of the first coins were made of very rare and expensive metals, like gold and silver. It was easy to carry a few coins that might be worth a whole cow or a day's work. These days few coins are actually made of rare and expensive metals. In fact, much of our money is made of paper.

A. Exercising Your Skill

Answer these questions about the paragraph you just read.

1. What is used to make most money today?

2. What must money have in order to make it work?

3. What could we use for trading if we didn't have money?

4. What was used to make some of the first coins?

5. What is one reason money is useful for spending rather than for trading?

B. Expanding Your Skill

United States presidents from the past are pictured on some coins and on paper money. Find out who some of these presidents are and which kinds of money their faces appear on. On your paper, make a list of the names you find. Beside each name write the name of the coin or bill that carries that president's picture.

C. Exploring Language

Look at the fronts and backs of three different coins. What words are printed on the front of every coin? Write the words on your paper. What words are printed on the back of every coin? Write these words. See if you can find out what the non-English words *E pluribus unum* mean. These words form a motto. Write what the motto means and what language it is printed in.

Now choose one coin, and write a description of it. Include details about its color, shape, and size, and about the pictures and words printed on it.

D. Expressing Yourself

Choose one of these activities.

1. Choose one of the kinds of funny money you learned about in Unit 5. It could be the cheese money of Russia, Malayan coins from the trunk of a tin-money tree, or some other kind of money. Write three or four sentences describing this money—what it is made of, what it looks like, and what you imagine it might have been worth in terms of what a person might have been able to get in exchange for it.

2. Role-play a trade with a partner. You have a certain kind of money (one of the kinds you read about or a kind you invent for the skit). Your partner has a product or service you want to buy. Act out how you would bargain with each other during this trading situation.

3. Design your own money system. What would the money be made of? What would it look like? Would your money system include something called coins, or would you call these things something else? What name would you give each coin? Draw pictures of the different kinds of money in your money system. Write a sentence or two about each picture, explaining what the money is and what its value is.

Unit 7
The Elephant Bird

The first people who visited Africa came back with strange stories. One of their stories was about a giant bird. The name of the bird was the "elephant bird."

The elephant bird was very large. One story told how it could eat baby elephants. Another story told how the bird would drop rocks on ships that passed. Still another story told of how the bird carried a person away in its claws! People liked to hear such stories, but not all of them were true. People began to wonder whether the elephant bird was real. "No bird could grow that large," people said.

Today we know for a fact that the elephant bird really did live. How do we know? Bones of the bird have been found. The bones were dug out of the ground on the island of Madagascar, off the east coast of Africa. Eggshells of the elephant bird have also been found.

The bones show that the elephant bird was a giant, taller than the tallest human being. It was ten feet tall. It was also very heavy. An elephant bird often weighed 1,000 pounds. The eggs of the elephant bird were the largest eggs ever laid—the size of basketballs. If people found the eggshells today, they could make them into water jugs. The jugs could hold more than eight quarts of water.

No one knows how the elephant bird got its name. We do know that it was too heavy to fly, so not all the stories about it are true. Do you have any idea why it was called the elephant bird?

Unit 7
The Elephant Bird

1. The elephant bird was said to eat
   (A) grass.   (B) baby elephants.   (C) horses.

2. The elephant bird was said to drop rocks on
   (A) homes.   (B) people.   (C) ships.

3. The stories about the bird were
   (A) disliked.   (B) all true.   (C) not all true.

4. Bones of the elephant bird have been
   (A) found.   (B) made.   (C) painted.

5. The elephant bird lived near
   (A) China.   (B) New York.   (C) Africa.

6. The elephant bird was taller than the tallest
   (A) human.   (B) tree.   (C) building.

7. The elephant bird weighed about
   (A) 1,000 pounds.   (B) 100 pounds.   (C) 2,000 pounds.

8. The egg of the elephant bird was as large as a
   (A) mountain.   (B) river.   (C) basketball.

9. Eggshells of the elephant bird could be used for
   (A) holding food.   (B) washing babies.   (C) water jugs.

10. No one knows how the elephant bird got its
    (A) nest.   (B) name.   (C) food.

Unit 8
Is Anything Down There?

What is it that swims in Loch Ness? No one knows. Those who have seen it call it the "monster." They have named it the "Loch Ness Monster."

Loch Ness is a long and very deep lake in Scotland. Since the year 565, many people there have told of seeing a strange animal with a long, snakelike neck and a small head. Most of those who have seen it say the Loch Ness Monster is dark, has a hump like a camel, and is about 50 feet long.

Some people have taken pictures of the beast. However, none of the pictures came out clearly, and one film that was said to be of the monster turned out to be a fake. But the pictures do seem to show a dark animal with a long neck, a small head, and a long body.

Some people think that the thing in Loch Ness is a rock or a log floating in the lake. "But how can a rock swim?" ask those who believe in the monster. "Besides, do rocks or logs have necks and heads?" Some say it is not a rock or a log but only a seal. Those who have seen the creature say that no seal ever grew that big. Scientists have taken pictures underwater but have found nothing.

Perhaps we will never know what it is that lives in the waters of Loch Ness. Maybe someday someone will get a clear photograph of the mysterious creature. Until that happens, what do you think the Loch Ness Monster is?

Unit 8
Is Anything Down There?

1. People have seen the monster since the year
(A) 1622.   (B) 1799.   (C) 565.

2. Loch Ness is in
(A) Scotland.   (B) Ireland.   (C) Canada.

3. The neck of the monster is said to be
(A) green.   (B) long.   (C) short.

4. People who see the monster say it has
(A) a huge head. (B) a small head.   (C) no head.

5. The length of the monster is said to be about
(A) 25 feet.   (B) 15 feet.   (C) 50 feet.

6. The pictures taken of the monster
(A) are clear.   (B) were never taken.   (C) are not clear.

7. Some people think that the monster is a
(A) rock.   (B) boat.   (C) person.

8. Other people say the monster is a
(A) giant bird.   (B) seal.   (C) snake.

9. Some people say it could not be a seal because a seal is
(A) dark.   (B) too big.   (C) much smaller.

10. Scientists took pictures underwater and found
(A) nothing.   (B) the Loch Ness Monster. (C) seals.

Everything about the hummingbird is small. The egg from which it is hatched is about the size of a jelly bean. The nest in which it is born is the size of a walnut. A baby hummingbird is only the size of a bee. When fully grown, it is only two inches long and weighs less than a penny. It weighs so little that it can stand on a blade of grass and the blade hardly bends!

No bird can match the hummingbird in flight. It can hang in midair without moving up or down, backward or forward. The long, strong wings move so quickly that they can hardly be seen. By studying them in slow motion, scientists know their wings beat more than 60 times each second. You can hear them. They make a humming sound. That is how the hummingbird got its name.

The hummingbird is as fast as it is small. It zips, dips, and darts at speeds greater than 50 miles an hour. It can fly backward or sideways and can rise straight into the air like a little rocket. The bird has been known to fly 500 miles without stopping for a rest.

The hummingbird is a fearless fighter. It will pick fights with birds of all sizes. It is as likely to go after a crow or a hawk as a moth or a bee. It will fly at its enemies like a bullet, using its sharp bill as a weapon.

Hummingbirds spend most of their time in the air. Their feet are weak and are not meant for walking. But then, a bird is born to fly—and no bird can fly like the little rocket of the airways, the hummingbird.

1. The hummingbird's egg is about the size of a
   (A) jelly bean.   (B) pea.   (C) watermelon.

2. The hummingbird's nest is the size of
   (A) an ant.   (B) a bird.   (C) a walnut.

3. The hummingbird weighs less than
   (A) a leaf.   (B) a penny.   (C) a drop of water.

4. The hummingbird's wings beat 60 times each
   (A) minute.   (B) hour.   (C) second.

5. The wings of the hummingbird make a
   (A) burning sound.   (B) humming sound.   (C) crying sound.

6. Hummingbirds can fly faster than
   (A) 50 miles per hour.   (B) lightning.   (C) airplanes.

7. Hummingbirds take nonstop flights of
   (A) fancy.   (B) 500 miles.   (C) 1,000 miles.

8. The hummingbird likes to
   (A) sing.   (B) walk.   (C) fight.

9. The hummingbird uses its pointed bill as a
   (A) spoon.   (B) bullet.   (C) weapon.

10. Of all the birds, the hummingbird is the best
    (A) worker.   (B) flyer.   (C) eater.

Unit 10
Island of the Past

Did you ever wonder what it was like to live in the olden days? There is a place called Mackinac Island where you can find out.

On this island, instead of "Beep, beep!" you hear "Clippety clop," "Giddyup!" and "Whoa!" on the streets. No automobiles are allowed. Many people ride in horse-drawn carriages. The people like it this way—just as it was in the olden days.

Mackinac Island is in the American Great Lakes. Many people spend summer vacations there because of the island's beautiful trees and sandy beaches. But they also go there to enjoy the old-fashioned life. They ride around in shiny black carriages pulled by pairs of handsome horses. These carriages look like stagecoaches in Western movies—only smaller. They have big wooden wheels, and the driver sits on top up front, holding the horses' reins. The driver wears a bright red coat and a black high hat.

Not everybody rides in carriages. Some people saddle up and ride horseback. Others pedal along on bicycles or just walk. Nobody seems to miss the cars.

Long ago only Native Americans lived on Mackinac. They believed it was the oldest island in the world. They said the island was created by piling earth on the back of a giant turtle. In the frontier days, hunters, trappers, and soldiers used Mackinac as an important base.

Today the people of Mackinac like to remember their past. They have repaired an old fort and many old houses and stores. One house is even older than the United States! The residents take visitors on tours through these old buildings and tell them about the olden days. If you ever want to return to the past, just take a trip to Mackinac.

Unit 10
Island of the Past

1. You could find out what life in the olden days was like at
   - (A) Rhode Island.
   - (B) Coney Island.
   - (C) Mackinac Island.

2. People ride in carriages pulled by
   - (A) horses.
   - (B) tractors.
   - (C) goats.

3. Mackinac Island is in the
   - (A) Great South Bay.
   - (B) Great Salt Lake.
   - (C) Great Lakes.

4. The driver of the carriage holds the
   - (A) wheels.
   - (B) horses' reins.
   - (C) saddle.

5. The driver wears a
   - (A) red hat.
   - (B) red coat.
   - (C) black coat.

6. Nobody seems to miss the
   - (A) trains.
   - (B) cars.
   - (C) trucks.

7. Native American legends say the island is the world's
   - (A) oldest.
   - (B) smallest.
   - (C) noisiest.

8. People on the island repaired
   - (A) an old bus.
   - (B) an old fort.
   - (C) an old rug.

9. One house is older than
   - (A) Canada.
   - (B) Russia.
   - (C) the United States.

10. The people show visitors
    - (A) movies.
    - (B) old buildings.
    - (C) shells.

Unusual Dinners and Snacks

Why don't you surprise your family? Just wait until the next time they ask what you want for dinner. Just say, "How about kangaroo-tail soup?" See what they say. They may be surprised to learn that this soup is sold in some stores.

Maybe members of your family are tired of always having the same kinds of meats. Tell them about buffalo meat. Quite a few people like the taste. There is baby octopus too. You can find fresh baby octopus in some fish stores.

Most people like to eat a little snack between meals. Perhaps you can get your family to buy snails, which come from France. You might want your snails as a bedtime snack. Frogs' legs, roasted grasshoppers, and ants are also eaten as snacks. If your family members agree to buy the ants, ask them to get the chocolate-covered kind. They are crunchy.

Will your family think that your taste is a little strange? If so, tell them about the food eaten by people of long ago. In times past, people ate fern plants, spiders, worms, and crunchy dandelions. Mouse pie was a favorite too. A bear's paw was a treat, though it had to be cooked a long time before it was tender enough to eat. People said it had a sharp taste!

Perhaps your friends would like to try new foods with you. The next time you get together, make a list, and see what you can find. Even if it's a strange food, you just might like it.

1. When your family asks what you want to eat,
   (A) say nothing.   (B) surprise them.   (C) laugh.

2. Kangaroo-tail soup is sold
   (A) all over the world. (B) in some stores.   (C) in one store.

3. Fresh baby octopus can be found in
   (A) a zoo.   (B) some fish stores. (C) America.

4. Snails that we buy for food come from
   (A) France.   (B) Italy.   (C) Japan.

5. A food people like for snacks is
   (A) bears' ears.   (B) camel's hump.   (C) frogs' legs.

6. Chocolate-covered ants are
   (A) large.   (B) crunchy.   (C) dirty.

7. People of long ago ate
   (A) tigers.   (B) butterflies.   (C) spiders.

8. Dandelions are said to be
   (A) crunchy.   (B) sour.   (C) bitter.

9. A bear's paw is said to have a
   (A) sharp taste.   (B) sweet taste.   (C) flat taste.

10. A bear's paw was made tender by
    (A) freezing it.   (B) cutting it.   (C) cooking it.

Unit 12
Going Up?

Humans have been using machines to lift heavy objects for more than 2,000 years. These first lifting machines used ropes and pulleys. They were powered by animals and humans. These were the world's first elevators.

Power from waterwheels came next. Then steam power was used. In 1880 the first electric elevator was made by Werner von Siemens. He was a German inventor.

Early elevators were used to lift things. The things were too big or heavy to carry. If the cable broke, the elevator would fall. Then Elisha Otis invented the safety elevator. It had a special brake. The brake would stop the elevator if it began to fall. His change made people feel safe when riding elevators. Now people everywhere wanted to use elevators.

In the 1880s the first skyscrapers were built. Many new inventions from the 19th century made these buildings possible. Steel was a new material. It was used to create a very strong framework. Heating and plumbing systems kept people comfortable. The telephone allowed them to talk without leaving their home or office. The lightbulb allowed them to see in the dark. But who would want to walk up and down 20 flights of stairs every day? The Otis Elevator made it practical for people to work and live in skyscrapers.

Many big cities around the world have skyscrapers, but it was Otis who made it possible for people to live and work in such tall buildings. The next time you ride an elevator, look for his name. The Otis Elevator Company still makes elevators today.

1. Who invented the electric elevator?
   (A) Elisha Otis
   (B) Werner von Siemens
   (C) ancient Egyptians

2. People have been using lifting machines
   (A) for thousands of years.
   (B) since 1880.
   (C) since 1950.

3. The first lifting machines used
   (A) ropes and pulleys.
   (B) safety brakes.
   (C) steam power.

4. **Elevator** is another word for
   (A) freight.
   (B) cable.
   (C) lifting machine.

5. What made people feel safe enough to ride an elevator?
   (A) a new kind of brake
   (B) electricity
   (C) skyscrapers

6. Which of these was *not* an invention of the 19th century?
   (A) steel
   (B) pulleys
   (C) telephones

7. When you ride an elevator today, whose name can you sometimes find?
   (A) Siemens
   (B) Otis
   (C) Edison

8. Without elevators, it would be very hard to live or work in
   (A) offices.
   (B) homes.
   (C) skyscrapers.

9. Who invented the "safety brake" for electric elevators?
   (A) Siemens
   (B) Otis
   (C) Edison

10. The biggest danger before the safety brake was that elevators would
    (A) stop.
    (B) fall.
    (C) spin.

In Unit 11 you read about many strange foods. Maybe you would prefer a sandwich. You can still find some really different foods in the everyday sandwich. Read about them in the paragraph that follows.

In almost every country, people serve food inside some kind of bread or pastry. Our typical sandwich—a piece of meat between two slices of bread—was invented in England. Peanut butter and bananas as a filling came much later! You may have had tacos—thin corn pancakes that have been fried and then wrapped around shredded meat. The people of Wales have given us meat pasties—a triangle of pastry with meat and vegetables baked inside. The Italians have provided calzones—bread baked around cold cuts and cheese. The Chinese or Vietnamese egg roll is a rice pancake wrapped around shreds of meat and vegetables and then fried.

A. Exercising Your Skill

Think of the foods you have read about. Which ones would you be willing to try? Which ones would you avoid? Read "Unusual Dinners and Snacks" in Unit 11 again, and then reread the paragraph above. Copy the following headings on your paper. List as many foods as you can think of under each heading.

Foods I Would Try	Foods I Would Avoid

B. Expanding Your Skill

What other foods can you think of? Which are your favorites? Choose one food that you haven't read about yet. On your paper, write a few sentences describing this food and why you like it. Also include a sentence that explains why you think other people should try this food.

C. Exploring Language

You know a lot about food. You know what people usually eat for breakfast, lunch, dinner, and snacks. Think about what you know from your own experience and from what you have read and seen on television. Imagine that you own a restaurant. What would be on the menu in your restaurant? Divide your menu into five sections. Then write the following headings on your paper. For each heading, list the names of four or five different foods.

Soups	Salads	Main Dishes	Vegetables	Desserts
___	___	_____	_____	_____
___	___	_____	_____	_____

D. Expressing Yourself

Choose one of these activities.

1. Imagine that you are going to interview a person who is known for being a good cook. This person might be someone in your family, a friend, a neighbor, or a cook in a local restaurant. Write a list of questions that you could ask this person. If possible, set up an actual interview with the person, and report to your class what you find out.

2. Role-play an interview with a partner who is pretending to be a famous cook. Make a list of questions to ask the famous cook. Your partner (the famous cook) can make up likely answers as you ask your questions.

3. Write a short story that tells about some experience you have had in which food played an important part. Did you have a week in which you ate the same food over and over again? Did you try some new food? Did you spill tomato sauce on your aunt's new tablecloth? Your story can be about a time that was odd, exciting, or funny.

Unit 13
Deer on the Doorstep

Would you be surprised to open your front door and find a 400-hundred-pound deer standing there? Would you think it odd to see two deer strolling down the middle of your town's busiest street? In most towns such sights would certainly be strange. In Waterton, Canada, they are common.

Every winter dozens of mule deer come into Waterton from the nearby hills and woods. They are called mule deer because they have long ears, like mules. The deer roam through the town. They cross lawns and climb onto porches. They walk down the middle of streets and even along sidewalks. At busy corners cars screech to a stop as the deer cross, paying no attention to traffic lights.

The people of Waterton are so used to the deer that they hardly notice them—until the animals start eating their trees and bushes. Unlike most deer, these mule deer are not at all afraid of people. They do not dash off when someone tries to shoo them away from eating a tree on a front lawn. This is the only thing the people of Waterton do not like about the deer. The deer eat so much bark and so many leaves that many lovely bushes and trees die. No garden in Waterton is safe.

Have you already figured out why the deer like to spend their winter vacations in Waterton? There is plenty of food there. In the mountains and forests, many deer die each winter because deep snow covers the grass and bushes they eat. The deer come to town for other reasons too. There they are safe from their natural enemies—mountains lions and coyotes. Also, they find warmer shelter behind houses.

The people of Waterton have learned to get along with the deer, even though the animals get in the way. The deer too have had to learn to put up with people who get in their way—all the visitors who come to Waterton to take their pictures!

Unit 13
Deer on the Doorstep

1. It might be strange to see two deer walking on
   (A) a kitchen floor. **(B)** a busy street. **(C)** a rooftop.

2. These sights are common in
   (A) Waterton. **(B)** Jollytown. **(C)** New York City.

3. The deer come from nearby
   (A) zoos. **(B)** kingdoms. **(C)** woods.

4. The deer do not watch
   (A) street signs. **(B)** crossing guards. **(C)** traffic lights.

5. The deer are not afraid of
   (A) mice. **(B)** fireworks. **(C)** people.

6. In Waterton the deer find plenty of
   (A) money. **(B)** soda. **(C)** food.

7. Besides mountain lions, enemies of the deer are
   (A) rabbits. **(B)** coyotes. **(C)** cats.

8. The deer find shelter behind
   (A) houses. **(B)** flowers. **(C)** buses.

9. People in Waterton have learned to get along with the
   (A) visitors. **(B)** children. **(C)** deer.

10. Visitors take the deer's
   (A) pictures. **(B)** toys. **(C)** mail.

Unit 14
Names, Names, Names

People like to give names to everything they see. They give names to towns, cities, streets, lakes, rivers, parks, and mountains. Some of the names are funny. Some are sad. Other names are just downright silly. We do not always know how names came to be chosen, but names dot our maps.

Sometimes the names of people are used to name places. There are places called David, Ruth, Nick, and Charles. Even the last names of people are used. Our country's capital is Washington, the name of our first president. There is a city called Lincoln. Other places have names as common as Smith and Jones.

Almost every animal has a place named after it. How would you like to live in a place called Buzzard's Bay? Or would Spider, Beaver, Black Snake, or Buffalo be more to your liking? Animals are favorites when it comes to naming places.

Would you like to live in a town with a happy name? New Hope, Sunrise, Beauty, Smile, and Good are pleasant names. Would you like to live in Lovely, Blessing, or Jollytown? All of these are names of places in our country. There are places with names that are not so happy. They are Worry, Strain, and Broken Arrow. Such names could hardly make us smile. There are also many silly names such as Stone, Busy, Hi Hat, Sparks, and Dime Box.

The longest name of a place in our country is Lake Chargogga-goggmanchaugagoggchaubunagungamaugg. It is a Native American word that means, "You fish on your side of the lake, and I'll fish on mine."

1. When people see things, they like to

    (A) draw them.   **(B)** name them.   **(C)** eat them.

2. One name that was used to name a place is

    (A) Tom.   **(B)** Bill.   **(C)** Nick.

3. Our nation's capital is named for

    (A) an animal.   **(B)** a person.   **(C)** Lincoln.

4. Places named after animals are

    (A) small.   **(B)** few.   **(C)** many.

5. When most people hear the name "Good," they

    (A) shudder.   **(B)** leave.   **(C)** smile.

6. A happy name found in the story is

    (A) Black Snake.   **(B)** Worry.   **(C)** Jollytown.

7. A sad name found in the story is

    (A) Smile.   **(B)** Broken Arrow.   **(C)** Tears.

8. A silly name found in the story is

    (A) No Money.   **(B)** Dancing Bear.   **(C)** Dime Box.

9. The longest name of a place in our country was given to

    (A) a fish.   **(B)** a lake.   **(C)** an island.

10. The longest name of a place in our country was thought of by

    (A) teachers.   **(B)** a Native American.   **(C)** swimmers.

Unit 15
Native American Feathers

Have you ever seen the feathers on a real Native American arrow? Have you ever taken a good look at them? If you have, you know that some of the feathers are marked. They may also be cut, split, or colored. Long ago, the Plains Indians wore these in different ways. Some wore their feathers straight up. Others wore them sideways or hanging down.

The markings and the ways the feathers were worn tell us a lot about the Plains Indians. Not many people today know what the markings mean. The feathers tell a story of what a warrior did in battle. They tell why the warrior had a right to wear them. Feathers were somewhat like medals.

Plains Indian warriors who were very brave in battle could wear a feather straight up. They had to kill an enemy or touch a live enemy in battle and escape. If anyone touched an enemy who was hurt and got away, they could wear a feather sideways. The first warrior to touch a dead enemy could wear a feather hanging down.

The colors and markings of each feather meant something too. For some groups the white feather showed that a warrior had killed an enemy. A red spot on a feather meant the same thing. A red feather showed that the warrior had been hurt in battle. A split feather showed that the owner had been hurt many times.

The next time you see a picture showing Plains Indians of long ago, look at the feathers they are wearing. What can you tell about them from their feathers?

Unit 15
Native American Feathers

1. You must look carefully at feathers to see how they are
   (A) marked.   (B) gathered.   (C) pinned.

2. Today few people know the meaning of
   (A) bird feathers.   (B) feather beds.   (C) Native American
                                                   feathers.

3. Feathers tell what the Plains Indians did in
   (A) camp.   (B) battle.   (C) school.

4. A warrior who touched an enemy who was hurt could wear a
   feather
   (A) sideways.   (B) backward.   (C) forward.

5. A feather hanging down meant that the wearer was the first to
   touch
   (A) a dead enemy.   (B) a friendly enemy. (C) an arrow.

6. To show that he had killed an enemy, the warrior wore a
   (A) white feather.   (B) purple feather.   (C) blue feather.

7. A spot on a feather meant a warrior had
   (A) killed an enemy. (B) been wounded.   (C) been in battle.

8. If a warrior had been hurt in battle, he wore a
   (A) bandage.   (B) red feather.   (C) green feather.

9. A warrior who had been wounded many times wore a
   (A) split feather.   (B) necktie.   (C) big feather.

10. Native American arrow feathers can tell
    (A) birds.   (B) stories.   (C) pens.

Unit 16
The Woman Who Wouldn't Give Up

It was 1838, and one of the worst storms in history was roaring along the coast of England. The lighthouse keeper looked out at a ship. "It will be gone in a few more minutes," he said sadly.

His daughter, Grace Darling, could see the scared people on the ship. "Can't we save them?" she asked. "Isn't there any way to help them?"

"No one can take a lifeboat out in that water," he answered. "The waves are too large."

Grace had great courage. She simply did not know how to give up. Filled with pity, she raced to the lifeboat. Her father followed. He pleaded with her not to get into the boat, but she would not listen. Her father could not let her go alone. He climbed in too. The two of them rowed frantically. Each wave seemed ready to hurl them into the sea.

Suddenly there was a terrible roar. The storm had split the ship in two. People were clinging to each half. They had to be rescued soon.

Grace and her father rowed faster. Soon they reached the ship and began filling the lifeboat with survivors. Then father and daughter brought their lifeboat safely to shore.

To this day a small statue stands above the grave of Grace Darling. Sailors from all over England visit it. People still honor the young woman who refused to give up.

Unit 16
The Woman Who Wouldn't Give Up

1. The storm took place in
   (A) 1900. (B) 1800. (C) 1838.

2. The storm roared along the coast of
   (A) France. (B) Ireland. (C) England.

3. The lighthouse keeper's daughter was named
   (A) Grace. (B) Mary. (C) Frances.

4. His daughter wanted to
   (A) help. (B) run. (C) swim.

5. Her father said the waves were too
   (A) fast. (B) large. (C) strong.

6. She was filled with
   (A) pity. (B) fear. (C) doubt.

7. She and her father
   (A) rowed. (B) called for help. (C) swam.

8. The ship
   (A) overturned. (B) sank. (C) split in two.

9. Grace and her father filled the lifeboat with
   (A) life jackets. (B) survivors. (C) oars.

10. Above the grave of the young woman who saved lives is a
    (A) lifeboat. (B) statue. (C) tree.

Unit 17
Lights in the Night Sky

Is there life on other planets? Do visitors from outer space fly over our cities and towns? Some people think so. But, of course, no one knows for sure.

People sometimes report seeing strange-looking lights in the night sky. Some believe the lights are spaceships. They say these spaceships give off light as they zoom through the sky. Some pilots have reported seeing small flying objects flash past their planes. They have said these objects look like dishes or saucers. That is where the term **flying saucers** came from.

In the last 50 years, thousands of people have seen these lights from the ground and from the air. Some have taken pictures of these flying saucers. They are said to fly much faster than airplanes and dart out of sight very quickly.

Many of these lights in the sky have been explained. Sometimes they are meteors, satellites, or weather balloons. Sometimes airplanes are even mistaken for flying saucers.

However, scientists say there could be life on some faraway planets. They say that whoever lives there could know more than we do on Earth. These life-forms could be ahead of us in technology. They could be curious about our world. Who knows? Maybe someday we will have a chance to answer these questions.

1. Some people say that the strange lights could be
   (A) pretty.   (B) spaceships.   (C) green.

2. The spaceships are said to look like
   (A) airplanes.   (B) people.   (C) saucers.

3. The lights have been seen by
   (A) few people.   (B) thousands of people. (C) nobody.

4. The flying objects are said to fly faster than
   (A) airplanes.   (B) light.   (C) kites.

5. The flying objects are said to be rather
   (A) small.   (B) large.   (C) ugly.

6. When some people hear about flying saucers, they are
   (A) doubtful.   (B) funny.   (C) bored.

7. Some of these lights in the sky are really
   (A) costly.   (B) slow.   (C) meteors.

8. Sometimes the flying saucers are really
   (A) dishes.   (B) birds.   (C) airplanes.

9. Scientists think there could be life on
   (A) other planets.   (B) the sun.   (C) the rainbow.

10. Whoever might live on other planets could be
    (A) tired.   (B) boring.   (C) curious about
                                                     Earth.

Unit 18
Up, Up, and Away

How would you like to fly to school? Would you like to zip through the air like a bird? Someday you may be able to do just that. All you would need is your flying belt. You would be able to fly anywhere with just the push of a button!

You can't get a flying belt yet, but the belts have been tested by the U.S. Army. The army thinks that soldiers with flying belts could jump over fences and fly across rivers.

The flying belt has a small jet engine that is strapped on a person's back. A small tank holds jet fuel. When you press a button, the engine sends out a strong blast of air that pushes against the ground. That push sends you into the air. The flying belt can take you as high as you want to go. You can even change your speed and direction. To land safely, you slowly cut down the force of the blast.

The flying belt could be used not only by the army. Lifeguards could zoom over the water and save people in no time at all. Firefighters could fly to a fire. The flying belt might even help people get to work more quickly.

The flying belt could be used for fun too. It would be light, small, and easy enough for anyone to use. If you would like to blast off into the future, start saving your money. You could be first in your neighborhood to have a flying belt.

Unit 18
Up, Up, and Away

1. Someday you might be able to fly like a bird with
    (A) a flying fish.   **(B)** a flying belt.   **(C)** fly paper.

2. Flying belts are still not ready to be
    (A) sold.   **(B)** tested.   **(C)** frozen.

3. Flying belts would help the army
    (A) eat.   **(B)** sleep.   **(C)** cross rivers.

4. A flying belt is strapped on a person's
    (A) back.   **(B)** bicycle.   **(C)** car.

5. You will go up when a strong blast of air pushes against the
    (A) wings.   **(B)** nose.   **(C)** ground.

6. To come down you just cut the force of the
    (A) words.   **(B)** wings.   **(C)** blast.

7. The flying belt could be used by
    (A) birds.   **(B)** doctors.   **(C)** lifeguards.

8. The flying belt would help people get to
    (A) work.   **(B)** the attic.   **(C)** the basement.

9. The flying belt could be used for
    (A) fun.   **(B)** work only.   **(C)** cooking.

10. If you would like a flying belt, start saving your
    (A) steam.   **(B)** money.   **(C)** friends.

Unit 19
A Special Stone

Diamonds are among the most valuable objects found in the natural world today. They have long been valued for their beauty. In the past they were also thought to have special powers. French and Italian kings once wore diamonds into battle. They thought these stones would keep them safe.

Where do people often see diamonds today? The most common place is in jewelry. Earrings and bracelets often have them. Many people like to use them in wedding rings. Some large diamonds are on display in museums. Others are locked up in bank vaults.

Diamonds are the hardest natural substance found on Earth. A diamond is so hard that it can be cut only by another diamond. Diamonds are not just used for their beauty. They are also used on tools. They make sharp tips on drill bits and saw blades.

Diamonds are found deep in Earth. They form when volcanoes erupt below Earth's surface. After the lava has cooled, it becomes igneous rock. Diamonds are found in this type of rock. Scientists think it takes millions of years for a diamond to be made.

Digging for and finding diamonds is called mining. South Africa is home to the richest diamond mines. Other countries in Europe and Asia also mine them. First the rough diamonds are mined. Then they are cut and polished. The most flawless diamonds are most valuable.

1. In the past, people believed diamonds
   (A) could float.   (B) were worthless.   (C) could keep
                                                   them safe.

2. Igneous rocks are formed by
   (A) volcanoes.   (B) glaciers.   (C) tornados.

3. Which country produces the most diamonds?
   (A) China   (B) South Africa   (C) The United States

4. Where do people usually see diamonds?
   (A) at the grocery store (B) in jewelry   (C) on clothing

5. To cut a diamond, you must use
   (A) a knife.   (B) an emerald.   (C) a diamond.

6. How long does it take to form a diamond?
   (A) hundreds of years (B) thousands of years (C) millions of years

7. The most valuable diamonds are
   (A) flawless.   (B) hard.   (C) round.

8. Diamonds can be used for
   (A) electricity.   (B) glass.   (C) drill bits.

9. Before they are used in jewelry, diamonds are
   (A) cut and polished. (B) washed and dried. (C) drilled and
                                                   hammered.

10. Diamonds are harder than
    (A) all plants.   (B) all rocks.   (C) all natural
                                                   substances.

In Unit 17 you read a story about flying saucers. Read these two paragraphs about flying saucers:

In the last 30 years, thousands of people have seen these lights from the ground and from the air. They have taken pictures of these flying saucers. The saucers are said to fly much faster than airplanes. They can dart out of sight very quickly and are often said to be rather small. Any creatures in them would have to be small too—perhaps only three or four feet tall.

Many people laugh when they hear of flying saucers. They say there are no such things. They say that flying saucers are just rays of light that have bounced from the ground into the air. Some people think they are light rays from the sun. Others believe they are rainbows, clouds, or maybe nothing at all.

A. Exercising Your Skill

What have people observed about flying saucers? Make up a fact list about flying saucers based on what you have just read. Divide your list into these two sections:

1. In Favor of Flying Saucers
2. Against Flying Saucers

Write the section headings on your paper. List at least three supporting facts—or facts that tell about the main idea or heading— under each heading.

B. Expanding Your Skill

Write a report that has two paragraphs. Use the headings and lists of facts you wrote for Part A. Turn each of the headings into a main idea sentence. Use the facts in supporting sentences. Then give your report a title. Compare your report with your classmates' reports. See how close their main idea sentences and facts are to yours.

C. Exploring Language

Imagine that you have seen something not easily believed—a flying saucer, a flying elephant, an alligator in the subway, a dragon, or anything else. First draw a picture of what you saw. Then write a paragraph describing the thing you saw. Include at least five facts in your description. Try to make the facts as believable as possible.

D. Expressing Yourself

Think about flying saucers and other hard-to-believe things. Then choose one of these activities.

1. Write a newspaper story about what you imagined in Part C. Use the facts you wrote and the picture you drew. Add any other information, such as the date and location, to make your event seem real.

2. Using the hard-to-believe thing you thought of or some other hard-to-believe thing or event, write a newspaper story explaining why it was not real. (The flying elephant, for instance, may actually have been a huge balloon in a parade!)

3. As you know, some people believe they have seen flying saucers, while other people think such things are ridiculous. When can you believe what you see? Magicians use special effects to make us "see" things that aren't there, or they can make things disappear that we thought we could surely see. What would convince you that something existed? Discuss this with a small group of your classmates. Work with them to make a list of the facts or ideas that would convince you and those in your group that something hard to believe really is true.

Unit 20
The Yeti

A Yeti is a creature that is part human and part beast. In fact, **Yeti** means "wild person of the mountains." People who live in Tibet believe in the Yeti. They tell strange stories about it.

There are even those who say they have seen a Yeti. They say it is about the size of a tall person. It is covered with reddish-brown hair. The face is flat like a monkey's. The head comes to a point. Most often the Yeti walks on two legs. When it is frightened, it runs on all fours. Its voice is loud and is often heard in the evening.

"How strange a Yeti must look!" visitors to Tibet say. "Is there really such a thing?" they ask. A few have gone to the high mountains of Tibet to find out. They want to get a look at the wild person of the mountains. Some people even hope to bring back a Yeti.

So far no one has been lucky enough to capture a Yeti. But large footprints have been found. Pictures of the tracks have been taken. They show that the Yeti has four toes and walks with bare feet in the mountain snow. Some people say these footprints are the tracks of a bear. Others say they are the tracks of a monkey. The people of Tibet say the tracks are made by the Yeti.

No one really knows who or what has made these tracks. No one even knows what a Yeti really is. Those who come from far away still look for the Yeti, but the people of Tibet do not. "After all," they say, "who in their right mind would want to get close to the wild person of the mountains?"

Unit 20
The Yeti

1. **Yeti** means "wild person of the
   (A) snow."
   (B) caves."
   (C) mountains."

2. A Yeti is said to be the size of a
   (A) dog.
   (B) tall person.
   (C) small person.

3. The hair of a Yeti is said to be
   (A) reddish brown.
   (B) black.
   (C) gray.

4. The face of a Yeti is supposed to be flat like that of a
   (A) horse.
   (B) monkey.
   (C) dog.

5. When a Yeti runs on all fours, it is said to be
   (A) frightened.
   (B) happy.
   (C) sad.

6. People say that a Yeti is often heard in the
   (A) morning.
   (B) afternoon.
   (C) evening.

7. The people who wish to find the Yeti go to
   (A) the zoo.
   (B) Tibet.
   (C) Spain.

8. So far a Yeti has not been
   (A) caught.
   (B) searched for.
   (C) talked about.

9. The pictures of the footprints show that the Yeti has
   (A) dirty feet.
   (B) four toes.
   (C) six toes.

10. Some people say that the tracks are those of
    (A) a bear.
    (B) an elephant.
    (C) a goat.

Unit 21
Queen of the Air

A huge crowd waited in silence. News of a tiny young woman had spread throughout New York. Lillian Leitzel announced that she would do a stunt called "the plange." In this stunt she would hold on to just one ring with one hand and whirl her entire body over her wrist. This was the most difficult stunt in the circus. Only the strongest people could do it. Few would even attempt it.

People watched intensely. The house was packed. Lights dimmed. Drums rolled, and cymbals crashed. Then Lillian began to hurl her body up into the air. It went right over her wrist. As she did, the audience began to pick up the count. They chanted in amazement, "One, two, three—." Still Lillian continued to whirl. At the count of 60 she stopped. The crowd rose to its feet. For 15 minutes they applauded wildly. In all of circus history, she was the first to do this dangerous stunt so many times.

An agent from Barnum and Bailey was present that night and signed her to a large contract. "Dainty Miss Leitzel," as she was called, became the biggest star in the world of the circus! She toured the world. She was the most famous circus act of the 1920s.

Lillian was very strong. She was also very small. She was only four feet seven inches tall. She could do 27 one-handed chin-ups! It is hard for most people to do even one.

Dainty Miss Leitzel became known as the "Queen of the Air." The plange was still her most famous act. She was once able to do 249 turns. She was graceful, strong, and brave. She married another circus star named Alfredo Codona. They toured the world together.

The Queen of the Air is one of the most famous circus acts of all time. Lillian was the first person ever elected into the Circus Hall of Fame.

1. The plange was a trick performed
   (A) from a ring.   (B) on a trampoline. (C) in the water.

2. When Lillian began to whirl, the audience
   (A) was silent.   (B) began to count.   (C) booed.

3. Lillian was called "Dainty Miss Leitzel" because
   (A) she was weak.   (B) she was tiny.   (C) she was shy.

4. How many one-armed chin-ups could Lillian do?
   (A) 15   (B) 27   (C) 60

5. The circus Lillian toured with was called
   (A) Alfredo's Circus. (B) Big Top.   (C) Barnum
                                                and Bailey.

6. Before Lillian did her act, there was a
   (A) drum roll.   (B) tiger act.   (C) cannon shot.

7. Why was Lillian famous?
   (A) She owned   (B) She was strong   (C) She was married
       the circus.   and graceful.   to a circus star.

8. Lillian Leitzel was the first person to
   (A) walk the tightrope. (B) spin from a ring. (C) be elected to
                                                 the Circus Hall
                                                 of Fame.

9. Her most famous trick was called
   (A) the dive.   (B) the plange.   (C) the roll.

10. In the 1920s, Dainty Miss Leitzel was
    (A) not famous.   (B) somewhat famous. (C) very famous.

Unit 22
The Dog That Thinks It's a Seal

A shiny black creature sees a fish 12 feet below the surface of the water. The creature dives, catches the fish in its teeth, and brings it to the surface. Is this creature a seal? No, it's a dog—the world's best swimming dog. Such dogs have been called "the dogs that think they are seals."

It's easy to guess the name of this kind of dog. It's called the "water dog." It comes from a country called Portugal (say "PORT you gull") across the ocean. For years and years the fishers of Portugal took water dogs along in their boats. These dogs helped the fishers in wonderful ways. They would jump into the water and herd the fish into the fishers' nets. If a fish escaped, a water dog would swim after it, catch the fish in its mouth, and bring it back to the net—without harming the fish.

The water dog can do even more amazing things. Its hind legs are so strong that it can leap right out of the water into a boat. It can swim from one fishing boat to another, carrying a message. In a war long ago, the Spanish navy used water dogs to swim from ship to ship with messages. An old, old story tells of a drowning sailor who was pulled from the sea and saved by a water dog.

Today, however, very few people know about the water dogs of Portugal. When the fishers got motorboats with radios, they didn't need their dogs as much. Nearly all the water dogs were forgotten. By 1960 there were only 50 water dogs left in the whole world.

Then an American named Mrs. Miller heard about the water dogs. She brought two of them to America. She took care of them and the puppies they soon had. Today there are many children and grandchildren of those two water dogs. They are gentle and make wonderful pets. You can buy one, but they are expensive. The average price for a water dog is $2,000.

1. The shiny black creature mentioned in the story is a

    (A) horse.   **(B)** dog.   **(C)** fish.

2. These animals think they are

    (A) farmers.   **(B)** monkeys.   **(C)** seals.

3. The fishers took their dogs in their

    (A) boats.   **(B)** trucks.   **(C)** stores.

4. The dogs would not harm the escaped

    (A) fisher.   **(B)** boat.   **(C)** fish.

5. A dog can swim between boats, carrying a

    (A) bottle.   **(B)** message.   **(C)** tale.

6. The sailor in the story was

    (A) singing.   **(B)** drowning.   **(C)** eating.

7. Instead of dogs, fishers began to use

    (A) radios.   **(B)** nets.   **(C)** telephones.

8. The number of water dogs in 1960 was

    (A) 50.   **(B)** 18.   **(C)** two.

9. The American woman who brought water dogs to America was named

    (A) Mrs. Farmer.   **(B)** Mrs. Fisher.   **(C)** Mrs. Miller.

10. The price of a water dog today is about

    (A) $100.   **(B)** $250.   **(C)** $2,000.

Unit 23
Harry Houdini

Harry Houdini could do almost anything. He could walk through a brick wall. He could escape from a trunk with a rope around it. He could even make an elephant disappear! Harry Houdini, you see, was a magician. He was not just a good magician. There has never been a magician like him.

Nearly any magician can make a rabbit disappear. Such an act was too easy for Harry Houdini. He used the biggest animal he could find—an elephant. Harry put the animal into a big box on the stage. A second later he opened the box and the elephant was gone! How did he do such a trick? Most people have no idea.

Maybe the Great Trunk Trick was his best. First Harry's hands were tied behind his back and he was put into a sack. Then the sack was tied and placed inside the trunk. The trunk was locked. Then ropes were put around it. Within a second Harry would pop out and take a bow. How the people clapped!

How could a person walk through a brick wall? The Great Houdini did it almost every day. He had the brick wall made right on the stage. People saw it being made. Small screens were then put on both sides of the wall. People stood on both sides of the brick wall to see that Harry did not go around it. Harry would stand on one side of the wall. In a second he would be on the other side. People could hardly believe their eyes.

Even today no one knows how Harry did all these tricks. They were only tricks. He said so himself. However, magicians never give away their secrets. Harry Houdini, the great magician, never did.

Unit 23
Harry Houdini

1. Harry Houdini could walk through a
   (A) needle.   (B) mountain.   (C) brick wall.

2. Harry Houdini made an elephant
   (A) cry.   (B) dance.   (C) disappear.

3. Houdini was a
   (A) movie star.   (B) magician.   (C) writer.

4. In the Great Trunk Trick, Harry's hands were
   (A) empty.   (B) tied.   (C) warm.

5. A rope was placed around
   (A) the trunk.   (B) Harry.   (C) the wall.

6. Houdini walked through a wall almost every
   (A) hour.   (B) day.   (C) year.

7. The brick wall was made on the
   (A) porch.   (B) ground.   (C) stage.

8. On both sides of the brick wall there were
   (A) people.   (B) bricks.   (C) rabbits.

9. Even today no one knows how Harry
   (A) did his tricks. (B) liked people.   (C) made the wall.

10. Magicians never give away their
    (A) money.   (B) secrets.   (C) rabbits.

Unit 24
Seagoing Bottles

Can you imagine finding a bottle with a message inside—or perhaps one containing money? Not long ago a child in New York found a bottle that had been washed up on the beach. Inside was $1,700. After waiting a year the youngster was allowed to keep the money.

Bottles sometimes contain notes from a person who is shipwrecked. A bottle was once found on a beach in Japan. Inside was a message. It read, "Thirty people and forty ponies are starving." It had been sent 200 years before. It had come to shore on a beach near the hometown of the person who had written the message!

Bottles may travel thousands of miles over the oceans. They may drift as far as 100 miles in a day. More than 50 years ago, a fisher placed a bottle into the North Sea just to see how far it would go. This bottle has been picked up many times. Each time it has been placed back into the water. It has circled the world five times!

Somewhere on the high seas may be the most valuable bottle of all. It contains a message written by a ship's captain. A storm was raging, and the captain feared the ship might go down. The captain placed a message into a bottle so that the world would know of the ship's difficulties. The message was addressed to the king and queen of Spain. If you are the finder, this message will be worth a fortune to you because it is signed by Christopher Columbus.

The next time you visit the beach, keep a close watch. You may find a bottle cast up on the sand. A seagoing treasure may have come home to rest.

1. Bottles sometimes contain

    (A) food.   **(B)** messages.   **(C)** maps.

---

2. The bottle found by the youngster in New York contained

    (A) $100.   **(B)** $1,700.   **(C)** $1,000.

---

3. The Japanese bottle arrived late by

    (A) 200 years.   **(B)** 100 years.   **(C)** 75 years.

---

4. In a single day a bottle may travel

    (A) 2 miles.   **(B)** 100 miles.   **(C)** 50 miles.

---

5. The fisher put the bottle into the North Sea

    (A) more than 50   **(B)** 20 years ago.   **(C)** 5 years ago.
    years ago.

---

6. This bottle has circled the globe

    (A) two times.   **(B)** three times.   **(C)** five times.

---

7. The captain feared the ship might

    (A) be late.   **(B)** be captured.   **(C)** sink.

---

8. The ship's captain wrote a message to the king and queen of

    (A) England.   **(B)** Portugal.   **(C)** Spain.

---

9. The message was signed by

    (A) Hernando Cortez.   **(B)** Christopher   **(C)** Myles Standish.
                              Columbus.

---

10. You may find a bottle washed up on the

    (A) sand.   **(B)** grass.   **(C)** street.

Unit 25
The Special Olympics

The Olympics are some of the most exciting sports events in the world. But there is another Olympics about which you may not have heard. This is the Special Olympics, for people with mental disabilities.

People with mental disabilities learn more slowly than other people. Sometimes they have trouble controlling the actions of their arms and legs. For years, many people thought that mentally disabled people could not take part in sports, but they were wrong.

The first Special Olympic Games were held in Chicago in 1968. One thousand people competed in many events. Since then Special Olympic programs have been organized in all 50 states and more than 150 countries. Today more than a million people participate in the Special Olympics.

Mentally disabled persons over the age of eight may take part in the Special Olympics. These people may also have physical disabilities. People have run in races using crutches or walkers. A young girl entered the long jump event with an artificial leg. A blind runner raced around the track with the help of his coach's voice. A deaf basketball team planned their plays using sign language.

Winning is wonderful for people who may never have had much success. But training for and entering the Special Olympics is also important. The participants become more confident. They learn how to concentrate in order to play well. Then they use that concentration in school to improve their schoolwork. Like anyone else they feel great when they prove they can do something well.

1. People with mental disabilities often learn
   (A) more slowly.   (B) quickly.   (C) walking.

2. No one thought people with mental disabilities could play
   (A) fair.   (B) sports.   (C) music.

3. The first Special Olympic Games were held
   (A) in 1968.   (B) last year.   (C) last century.

4. They were held in
   (A) Canada.   (B) all the states.   (C) Chicago.

5. Today the number of people taking part is more than
   (A) one million.   (B) 1,000.   (C) 10,000.

6. In order to take part, a person must be at least
   (A) 21.   (B) a teenager.   (C) eight.

7. People have entered races using
   (A) cars.   (B) crutches.   (C) skates.

8. A girl with an artificial leg entered the event called
   (A) swimming.   (B) the long jump.   (C) basketball.

9. A deaf basketball team planned its plays using
   (A) sign language.   (B) lip reading.   (C) hearing aids.

10. The Special Olympics helps mentally disabled people become
    (A) isolated.   (B) arrogant.   (C) confident.

Unit 20 told about the Yeti, the wild person of the mountains of Tibet. Read this story about a wild person—or thing—that's a bit closer to home.

For almost 200 years, the story has gone around concerning a giant human—or ape—or bear—that lives in the northwestern part of our continent, near the coast. The local word for the creature is *Sasquatch,* which means "wild person of the woods." Another name is Bigfoot.

One man, Albert Ostman, claims he was carried away by a Sasquatch in 1924. He was camping when a huge creature grabbed him, sleeping bag and all, and carried him 30 miles to a clearing in the woods. There Ostman was astonished to see a whole family of Sasquatch. After a week, Ostman escaped. He didn't tell anyone right away because he knew no one would believe him. When he did finally talk, Ostman said that the Sasquatch was between seven and eight feet tall. It had a square head and very long arms and was covered with hair. The members of the Sasquatch family could talk with each other, but Ostman did not know the language.

No one agrees about what Sasquatch is, or even if it exists, but at least 100 people claim to have seen the creature since 1920.

A. Exercising Your Skill

Imagine that you have come face-to-face with a Sasquatch. Draw a picture of what you might have seen. Use the facts in the story above to help you.

B. Expanding Your Skill

Read again about the Yeti in Unit 20. Make a list of the ways in which the Yeti and a Sasquatch are similar. Then make a list of the ways in which they are different. Compare your two lists with your classmates' lists.

C. Exploring Language

Imagine that you are a Sasquatch. You have been captured by some campers in the Rocky Mountains. What do you see? What do the campers look like? What are your feelings? Write a report that your other Sasquatch friends would believe.

D. Expressing Yourself

Choose one of these activities.

1. Put on a skit with a classmate. One of you takes the part of the Yeti. The other takes the part of a Sasquatch. Both of you have seen, in the distance, a small figure. The figure walks upright. It has very thick feet and wrinkled skin. When it gets warm, it takes some of the skin off! Its footprint shows no toes at all, but it leaves a funny pattern in the mud. What is the creature? Is it a small Yeti ancestor? Is it a young Sasquatch playing tricks? Could it be a new kind of bear? Or is it one of those creatures from the legend of the humans? Have a friendly argument about what you have seen. Make up your own explanations for the strange feet, skin, and so on.

2. Imagine that no one has ever seen an elephant. A friend comes back from a trip to the zoo—or to Africa. He or she claims to have seen a huge gray animal. It has a long nose that reaches the ground. It has legs like tree trunks. Two of its teeth grow out of the side of its mouth and are each three feet long! How would you respond? How would you "explain" each of the things your friend has seen? Write what you would say to your friend. You may want to present the friend's description and your response, or explanation, as a skit.